Dear Educators, Parents, and Caregivers,

Welcome to Penguin Core Concepts! The Core Concepts program exposes children to a diverse range of literary and informational texts, which will help them develop important literacy and cognitive skills necessary to meet many of the Common Core State Standards (CCSS).

The Penguin Core Concepts program includes twenty concepts (shown on the inside front cover of this book), which cover major themes that are taught in the early grades. Each book in the program is assigned one or two core concepts, which tie into the content of that particular book.

Beautiful Ballerinas covers the concept The Arts. This book can be used to expose students to informational text, as recommended in the CCSS for English Language Arts and Literacy. The Arts help students learn to appreciate, comprehend, and describe things and experiences with varied and rich language, which also are literacy skills outlined in the CCSS. Additionally, the concept in this book can be used as a springboard for writing tasks or to teach unfamiliar vocabulary. After you've read the book, here are some questions/ideas to get your discussions started:

- What art form is discussed in this book? Why is it considered an art form?

- This book contains a lot of unfamiliar vocabulary, such as *adagio*, *plié*, *reverence*, and *tendu*. Discuss the meaning of the words, and write new sentences using each one.

Above all, the books in the Penguin Core Concepts program have engaging stories with fantastic illustrations and/or photographs, and are a perfect way to instill the love of reading in a child!

Bonnie Bader, EdM
Editor in Chief, Penguin Core Concepts

Beautiful Ballerinas

by Elizabeth Dombey
illustrated by Shelagh McNicholas *and with photos*

Grosset & Dunlap
An Imprint of Penguin Group (USA) LLC

To all aspiring budding ballerinas!—SM

GROSSET & DUNLAP
Published by the Penguin Group
Penguin Group (USA) LLC, 375 Hudson Street, New York, New York 10014, USA

USA | Canada | UK | Ireland | Australia | New Zealand | India | South Africa | China

penguin.com
A Penguin Random House Company

Photo credits: front and back cover: © Comstock/Thinkstock; page 1: © Comstock/Thinkstock; page 3: © Hemera/Thinkstock; page 5: © liquidlibrary/Thinkstock; page 7: Pixland/Thinkstock; page 8: (Ballet teacher training a group of children) © Purestock/Thinkstock, (Ballet Dancers) © Fuse/Thinkstock; page 12: © Hemera/Thinkstock; page 14: © Goodshoot/Thinkstock; page 15: © Goodshoot/Thinkstock; page 17: © Goodshoot/Thinkstock; page 19: © iStockphoto/Thinkstock; page 20: © iStockphoto/Thinkstock; page 21: © Pixland/Thinkstock; page 24: © Creative Commons Attribution-Share Alike 3.0 Unported; page 25: © iStockphoto/Thinkstock; page 26: © iStockphoto/Thinkstock; page 27: public domain; page 28: public domain; page 29: public domain; page 30: © iStockphoto/Thinkstock.

Text copyright © 2014 by Diane Muldrow. Illustrations copyright © 2014 by Shelagh McNicholas. Published by Grosset and Dunlap, a division of Penguin Young Readers Group, 345 Hudson Street, New York, New York 10014. GROSSET & DUNLAP is a trademark of Penguin Group (USA) LLC. Manufactured in China.

Library of Congress Cataloging-in-Publication Data is available.

ISBN 978-0-448-46714-6 (pbk)   10 9 8 7 6 5 4 3 2 1
ISBN 978-0-448-47791-6 (hc)   10 9 8 7 6 5 4 3 2 1

It's an evening at the ballet, and excitement is in the air! As the orchestra begins playing music, the curtain rises.

At the center of the stage is a beautiful ballerina, wearing a white *tutu*. How graceful she is as she twirls around!

At the end of the ballet, the dancers take their elegant bows. The audience cheers and claps. Some people toss roses onto the stage.

But the life of a ballerina is more than wearing *tutus* and getting applause. To be the best, these dancers must work and study very hard. And they have done this since they were your age—or younger!

A ballerina may look delicate, but she is very strong. She needs her strength to hold herself up on one foot while her arms are lifted . . .

and to leap high in the air . . .

and to turn many times without falling!

A ballerina has to be flexible as well as strong to lift her leg so high. Her flexibility also protects her from getting hurt while she's moving quickly.

How does a ballerina become so strong and flexible? Every day, even the most famous ballerinas take ballet classes.

A ballet class begins at the *barre*. Dancers stand at the *barre* and exercise one side of their bodies at a time.

In ballet, there are five basic positions of the feet. Here they are:

First Position   Second Position   Third Position

Fourth Position   Fifth Position

Can you match your feet to each position? Now you are learning basic ballet!

There are five positions of the arms, too:

First Position

Second Position

Third Position

Fourth Position

Fifth Position

Now match your arms to the pictures.

Here are four exercises that take place at the *barre*, using the positions you've just learned. Now you will learn some French words!

The first exercise is called a *plié* (say: plee-AY).

The second exercise is called a *tendu* (say: tahn-DOO).

The third exercise is called *battement dégagé* (say: bat-MAHN day-ga-ZHAY).

And the fourth exercise
is called a *rond de jambe*
(say: rawn duh ZHOM).

Now the dancers leave the *barre* to do their center floor work. The exercises here are similar to the ones at the *barre*. First the dancers do a series of slow, graceful movements called *adagio* (say: ah-DAH-joh). During *adagio*, the dancers concentrate on the lines they are making with their legs, arms, and back.

Now on to the *allegro* (say: ah-LEG-roh) portion of class! The music picks up, and the dancers perform faster, livelier steps, such as turns and small jumps.

Then it's time for *grand allegro*, which is a series of large jumps.

Class is nearly over, and now the dancers gather for *reverence*.
They bow to show respect to their teacher and pianist, and to celebrate
the elegance of ballet.

Have you ever wondered how a ballerina is able to dance on tiptoe? She appears to be floating on air!

The secret to a ballerina's magical lightness is her satin *pointe* shoes.

Pointe shoes are delicate on the outside but sturdy on the inside. At the inside tip of the shoe is a stiff box, made of fabric and cardboard glued together. Since a dancer's body weight rests on the hard little platform at her toes, it's very important that the slipper fits her perfectly. A ballerina's *pointe* shoe is made by hand, just for her.

Pointe shoes are expensive, but they don't last very long. Sometimes, if the ballet is difficult, the shoes last only one performance. A ballerina may go through more than one hundred pairs of *pointe* shoes in a season!

Ballerinas haven't always worn *pointe* shoes. Did you know that ballet began in Italy over five hundred years ago? It was soon popular in nearby France, too.

The earliest ballet dancers were lords and ladies, kings and queens. Their "stage" was in a castle, perhaps at a wedding or ball. And their shoes weren't slippers—they had heels!

King Louis XIV reigned over France during the 1600s. He loved the formal steps of ballet, along with its beautiful music, costumes, and sets. When he was young, the king even performed many roles himself.

In 1661, the king founded the Royal Academy of Dance. The school was the first in the world where dance was studied seriously.

Ballet changed as the years passed. In the 1800s, dancers wanted to appear "lighter than air" onstage. To dance more easily on the tips of their toes, they began to pad the toes of their slippers. Soon Italian shoemakers made harder shoes using paper, satin, and heavy cloth called burlap, and the *pointe* shoe was born.

Maria Taglioni was a famous Italian ballerina who danced *en pointe* in the early 1830s. At that time, it wasn't considered proper for women to show their legs. Maria Taglioni shocked people when she shortened her ballet costume's long, flowing skirt to show off her beautiful *pointe* work. But soon a shorter and stiffer *tutu* was worn by all ballerinas.

Tutus weren't the only things in ballet to change.

The way a ballet dancer looked changed over time, too. When Russian ballerina Anna Pavlova was a student in 1891, most ballet dancers had small and compact bodies. Not Anna. She was teased by the other students for the way she looked. Her long, thin arms and legs earned her the nickname "The Broom."

Ballet training didn't come easily to Pavlova, but she worked hard and didn't give up. In 1905 she created the role of the Dying Swan, one of the most famous ballet roles to this day. It quickly made her famous.

Pavlova became one of the greatest ballerinas in history. She was the first ballerina to tour the world, and she inspired thousands of little girls across the United States to take ballet classes.

Do you ever wish you could dance in your very own pair of *pointe* shoes?

Before that day comes, you'll need several years of ballet training to make sure that your legs, feet, and ankles are strong enough for you to be able to dance way up on your toes. That may be when you are thirteen years old or so.

Would you like to start dancing right now? Practice the basic positions you learned earlier in the book, and then you can try this combination.

1. *Plié* (say: plee-AY): to bend. Put your feet and arms in First Position. Bend your knees. They should be directly over your toes.

2. *Relevé* (say: ruhl-VAY): to rise. Begin in First Position. While keeping your knees straight, lift your heels until all of your weight is centered on the balls of your feet.

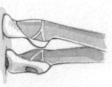

3. *Sauté* (say: soh-TAY): to jump. Begin in First Position, and then *plié*. Jump off with both of your feet at the same time and land on both feet at the same time. Land in a *plié* to cushion the knees.

If you can do these steps, you are on your way to becoming a beautiful ballerina!